IMAGES
of Aviation

NAVAL AIR STATION
PATUXENT RIVER

Mark A. Chambers

ARCADIA
PUBLISHING

Published by Arcadia Publishing
Charleston, South Carolina

Printed in the United States of America

Library of Congress Control Number: 2014936527

For all general information, please contact Arcadia Publishing:
Telephone 843-853-2070
Fax 843-853-0044
E-mail sales@arcadiapublishing.com
For customer service and orders:
Toll-Free 1-888-313-2665

Visit us on the Internet at www.arcadiapublishing.com

This pictorial history is dedicated to the personnel (both past and present) of the Naval Air Station Patuxent River, who worked and are working hard to help forge America's naval air arm.

CONTENTS

ACKNOWLEDGMENTS

The author would like to thank several individuals who helped to make this pictorial history a reality. I would like to thank my wife, Lesa, stepdaughter, Caitlyn, and son, Patrick, for enduring endless conversations regarding the subject matter of this book and for their constant encouragement and support. I would also like to thank my father, Joseph R. Chambers, for serving as a technical consultant and reviewer of this work as well as making several research trips with me to the US National Archives at College Park, Maryland.

Many thanks go to Holly Reed and the staff of the US National Archives at College Park, Maryland, Still Pictures Branch for photographic support for this project, and to Tim Neninger and the staff of the US National Archives at College Park, Maryland, Textual Reference Branch for documentation and additional photographic support for this project. In addition, thanks go to Connie Hempel (NAS Patuxent River HQ Public Affairs Officer), Kelly Burdick (NAVAIR), and Sarah Shenk (F-35 JSF Program, Lockheed Martin Corporation) for photographic support and approvals.

Special thanks also go to Julia Simpson of Arcadia Publishing for securing publication of this work, and for Sharon McAllister of Arcadia Publishing for her invaluable editorial assistance and dedicated support for this project.

INTRODUCTION

For the past 72 years, the Naval Air Station (NAS) Patuxent River, Maryland, has served as a flight-testing and evaluation stalwart of American naval aviation. NAS Pax River, home of the Naval Air Warfare Center, Aircraft Division (NAWCAD) and United States Naval Test Pilot School (TPS), as well as headquarters for NAVAIR, serves as the Navy's premier flight-test and evaluation center and is the Navy's equivalent of the US Air Force's Flight Test Center at Edwards Air Force Base (AFB) in Edwards, California. Much like Edwards AFB, Pax River is located in a secluded place, far away from heavily populated areas, making it ideal for flight-testing of advanced aircraft and aircraft weapons systems. Over the years, NAS Pax River has played a vital role in the development of naval aviation, conducting important tactical and operational feasibility and suitability testing for aircraft and aircraft weapons systems intended for fleet service. Throughout its history, NAS Pax River has also served as a center for foreign aircraft evaluations, particularly during and immediately following World War II. Some of the world's best test pilots, several of whom became astronauts, flocked to NAS Pax River to test-fly naval aviation's finest aircraft.

Today, NAS Pax River is helping America to maintain a technological edge over traditional and potential adversaries by conducting important flight-testing and evaluations of technologically advanced aircraft and aircraft weapons systems. Pax River also conducts important aircraft developmental ground tests in such unique facilities as the Air Combat Environment Test and Evaluation Facility (ACETEF) for simulated air combat and electronic warfare. ACETEF also houses a large anechoic chamber for evaluating electromagnetic environmental effects on aircraft and spacecraft. In addition, the naval air station features air vehicle/materials labs that routinely study and test new adhesives, landing-gear components, and organic coatings. In effect, NAS Pax River is continuing to help modernize America's naval air arm to 21st-century technological standards and keep the nation a step ahead of potential adversaries.

NAS Pax River was built in 1942 on a 6,400-acre stretch of farm properties located at Cedar Point, St. Mary's County, in southern Maryland. Civilization was sparse at the time, making the site ideal for performing the station's important mission—flight-testing and evaluating new aircraft and aircraft weapons systems. Many of the area's historically significant homes are now occupied by Navy servicemen and servicewomen and their families. One of Cedar Point's main tourist attractions for many years was the Cedar Point Lighthouse. In addition, the naval air station's grounds include some of the nation's most beautiful wildlife preserves and wetlands along the shores of the Patuxent River and Chesapeake Bay. Solomon Island, located across the Patuxent River from the naval air station, serves as a scenic getaway location for a multitude of people, including prominent politicians from Washington, DC.

Following America's entry into World War II, the Navy felt a tremendous need to consolidate some of the naval flight-testing and evaluation duties performed at NAS Anacostia, District of Columbia, and NAS Norfolk, Virginia, and relocate these functions to a new site, NAS Patuxent River, Maryland. This would relieve these stations from the increased workload spurred by the war. Ground was broken for NAS Pax River on April 4, 1942. During the war, developmental flight-testing and evaluation of important Navy aircraft, such as the Grumman F6F Hellcat and Vought F4U Corsair, were carried out at Pax River. The country's first combat operational unmanned aerial vehicle (UAV), the Interstate TDR-1, was flight-tested and evaluated at NAS Pax River. Pax River also achieved a first for naval aviation when it successfully flight-tested and evaluated the nation's first practical helicopter, the Sikorsky HNS-1 Hoverfly, in 1944. Some of the country's finest test pilots were given the opportunity to test-fly both Allied and captured Axis aircraft at the Joint Fighter Conference of 1944, held at Pax River. Important flight-testing and evaluation of foreign aircraft, which ultimately benefited US military and industry aviation planners, was carried out at the naval air station during and immediately following the war.

After World War II, the US Navy officially entered the jet age, and NAS Pax River contributed heavily to the development of jet-powered carrier aviation and America's eventual involvement in the Korean War. In 1946, the Naval Air Test Center (NATC) was established at Pax River. The station conducted important flight-testing and evaluation of advanced propeller-driven aircraft as well as the Navy's first carrier-based jet aircraft. In addition, testing and evaluation of aircraft weapons systems, including advanced UAVs, also took place at the naval air station. New aerial combat tactics were developed through flight-testing of jet aircraft at Pax River. Advanced rotorcraft were also routinely test-flown and evaluated at the naval air station. In the latter 1940s, the United States Test Pilot School (TPS) was established at NAS Pax River.

NAS Pax River was a key facilitator of the advent of the modern jet age and a major contributor to the American war effort in Vietnam. Once again, Pax River conducted important flight-testing and evaluation of advanced propeller-driven aircraft and modern Navy and Marine Corps jet aircraft, such as the Grumman F-14 Tomcat and the McDonnell Douglas F-4 Phantom II. Advanced aircraft weapons systems were tested and evaluated, and new air-combat tactics using modern jet aircraft were devised. Naval and Marine Corps rotorcraft flight-testing and evaluation continued, while advanced trainers were introduced into the TPS fleet.

From 1976 to 1999, NAS Pax River helped America win the Cold War against the Soviet Union and the Warsaw Pact and establish superpower supremacy. During this period, NAS Pax River conducted important flight-testing and evaluation of advanced Navy jet aircraft, propeller-driven aircraft, advanced aircraft weapons systems, advanced rotorcraft, advanced TPS aircraft, and advanced UAVs. Pax River also developed unique ground-based aerial combat simulators, anechoic chamber aircraft environment test facilities, and advanced aircraft structures and materials laboratories. NAWCAD and NAVAIR headquarters were also established at Pax River during this era.

From 2000 to 2014, NAS Pax River has worked to help modernize America's naval air arm to 21st-century technological standards and keep the nation a step ahead of potential adversaries. This has been accomplished through flight-testing and evaluation of advanced US Navy jet aircraft, including the F/A-18E and F Super Hornet, the EA-18G Growler, and stealthy F-35C Lightning II Joint Strike Fighter; advanced rotorcraft, such as the V-22 Osprey tilt-rotor wonder; and advanced UAVs, such as the jet-powered X-47B Unmanned Combat Air System (UCAS).

One

CEDAR POINT/ST. MARY'S COUNTY HISTORY
THE FOUNDATION OF A NAVAL AVIATION LEGACY

The Cedar Point/St. Mary's County land territories of southern Maryland are some of the most beautiful in North America. Prior to the establishment of Naval Air Station Patuxent River at Cedar Point in 1942, the area comprised 6,400 acres of rural farmland and served as the home of the Mattapany, Susquehanna, and Cedar Point farms. Several vacation homes belonging to wealthy homeowners also dotted the landscape.

Mattapany was named in honor of its first inhabitants, the Mattapanient Indians. The Mattapany farmhouse was erected in the latter portion of the 18th century and is now occupied by the commander of Naval Air Systems Command. Several historically significant homes in Cedar Point are now occupied by Navy servicemen and servicewomen supporting NAS Patuxent River and their families. The Cedar Point Lighthouse served as one of Cedar Point's main tourist draws for several years before being demolished in 1981.

Prior to the naval air station's establishment, civilization in Cedar Point was sparse, featuring just a few churches, a gas station, and a post office. With the establishment of the naval air station, the Cedar Point community experienced tremendous growth. Today, the community is sprawling with activity.

Before 1942, the main sources of income for Cedar Point residents were agriculture, fishing, and crabbing. With the establishment of NAS Patuxent River, the main source of income for residents became defense-related work performed in support of naval air station operations.

The Cedar Point/St. Mary's County area continues to pique the interests of many prominent Americans. Solomon Island, located across from the naval air station, continues to serve as a vacation destination for numerous prominent political officials in Washington, DC. Over the years, NAS Patuxent River has served as the home of some of the nation's prettiest wildlife preserves. In early July 1996, Pres. Bill Clinton visited one of these highly regarded preserves at the naval air station and successfully released a rehabilitated American bald eagle named Freedom.

Susquehanna Farmhouse. The Susquehanna House property featured a large farm. In 1942, Henry Ford acquired the house and transferred it, piece by piece, to his property in Dearborn, Michigan. (US Navy.)

Mattapany. Named in honor of its territorial inhabitants, the Mattapanient Indians, the Mattapany House was erected in the late 18th century. The house is presently occupied by the commander of Naval Air Systems Command and his family. (US Navy.)

CEDAR POINT LIGHTHOUSE. The Cedar Point Lighthouse is seen here four years prior to its demolition in 1981. Erected in 1894, the lighthouse became operational in 1896. Cedar Point was the sole remaining house-type light on Chesapeake Bay. The lighthouse was a tourist attraction for many years and was recognized as a historic site but deemed too decrepit for preservation. Upon the structure's demolition, the cupola was transferred to the Patuxent Naval Air Station Base Museum in 1982. (US National Archives, Still Pictures Branch.)

FLIGHT OF FREEDOM. In early July 1996, Pres. Bill Clinton (right) visited the Naval Air Station Patuxent River Wildlife Preserve and successfully released a rehabilitated American bald eagle, America's enduring icon, appropriately named Freedom. (US Navy.)

Two

Birth of an American Flight-Test and Evaluation Stalwart, World War II
1942–1945

After the Japanese surprise attack on US military installations on the Hawaiian island of Oahu on December 7, 1941, the US Bureau of Aeronautics demanded and received approval for the construction of a new naval air station whose primary function would be to flight-test and evaluate aircraft and aircraft weapons systems intended for fleet service. This critical station would take over some of the increased flight-testing and evaluation duties being handled by naval air stations and installations at Dahlgren and Norfolk, Virginia; the Washington Navy Yard; the Naval Aircraft Factory in Philadelphia; and Anacostia in Washington, DC. This heavy burden was brought on by America's formal entry into World War II.

The new facility became known as the Naval Air Station Patuxent River, Maryland, and construction commenced on April 4, 1942. Formal operations at the station began on April 1, 1943. As stated by the chief of the Bureau of Aeronautics, operations were commenced so that "aircraft and equipment developed elsewhere could be flown, tested, and criticized."

NAS Pax River was well suited to perform its critical mission. The naval air station featured four runways, numerous flight hangars, three seaplane basins, and an array of laboratories and shops.

From 1944 to 1946, NAS Pax River performed invaluable flight tests and evaluations of foreign aircraft, including both Allied and captured Axis aircraft, to determine their superior and inferior characteristics. In 1944, some of the world's best test pilots, including engineering test pilots from the National Advisory Committee for Aeronautics' (NACA) Langley Memorial Aeronautical Laboratory (LMAL), the world's premier civilian-led aeronautics research organization, came to Pax River to participate in the Joint Fighter Conference.

In the last few years of World War II, NAS Pax River tested the newest naval fighters and bombers, as well as their weapons and payloads. The naval air station also tested and evaluated enormous flying boats, America's first jet fighters, and America's first practical helicopter, making this unique facility a key player in establishing Allied naval air supremacy during and following World War II.

NAVALIZED "GOONEY BIRD." In February 1942, this Navy Douglas R4D-1, a navalized version of the Army's famous C-47 Skytrain, or "Gooney Bird," arrived at the flying field that was to become Naval Air Station Patuxent River, Maryland. The R4D-1 was one of the first aircraft, and the first military transport, to arrive at the flying field, bringing important Navy flight-test personnel and officials to the future naval air station site. (US National Archives, Still Pictures Branch.)

ROYAL AIR FORCE GRUMMAN "GOOSE." This British Royal Air Force (RAF) Grumman JRF-6B "Goose" navigation trainer and air-sea rescue amphibian flying boat arrived at the Pax River flying field in February 1942. The aircraft was test-flown and evaluated by American flight-test personnel. Several examples of the aircraft type were provided to the British by the United States under the Lend Lease Act. The RAF Geese fished many downed RAF fighter pilots, defending the skies over England from German raiders during the Battle of Britain and the ensuing blitz, out of the English Channel. (US National Archives, Still Pictures Branch.)

CATALINA PROTOTYPE. This Consolidated PBY-5A Catalina flying boat prototype arrived for flight-testing and evaluation at Pax River in early March 1942. Note the Yagi anti-shipping radar detection antennae under the wing and on the fuselage sides of the aircraft. Fleet operational versions of this type of aircraft successfully detected and spotted the Japanese carrier task force during the Battle of Midway, the pivotal battle of the Pacific in World War II that turned the tide of the war. (US National Archives, Still Pictures Branch.)

CATALINA PROTOTYPE. The PBY-5A Catalina Prototype performs initial flight trials above Pax River in early March 1942. (US National Archives, Still Pictures Branch.)

AVENGER PROTOTYPE IN FLIGHT. The Grumman TBF-1 Avenger torpedo bomber prototype is seen during flight- and fleet-acceptance trials over Pax River in late March 1942. The Avenger first saw combat during the Battle of Midway and did not get off to a good start, as an attacking force of eight unescorted Avengers carried out an unsuccessful attack on the Japanese carrier task force in the waters off Midway Island. Only one badly damaged Avenger managed to make it back to Midway, the planes being badly mauled by Japanese Zero fighters. Following the debacle at Midway, the Avenger became a workhorse for the Navy, wreaking significant damage on Japan's naval and shipping fleets, naval air and army air force bases, and troop fortifications and installations. The aircraft proved to be one of World War II's finest torpedo bombers. (US National Archives, Still Pictures Branch.)

WILDCAT PROTOTYPE. A Grumman F4F-7 Wildcat prototype at the flying field at Pax River awaits initial flight- and fleet-acceptance trials in April 1942. US Marine Corps ace and test pilot Marion E. Carl flew the aircraft type as a member of the famous Cactus Air Force that so gallantly defended Henderson Field on Guadalcanal against constant Japanese air raids during the Battle of Guadalcanal in late 1942. The Wildcat came out almost even with the seemingly invincible Japanese Mitsubishi A6M2 Type 21 Zero in aerial combat, although the Zero held a slight edge over the Wildcat in terms of maneuverability. (US National Archives, Still Pictures Branch.)

MARINE CORPS ACE AND TEST PILOT MARION E. CARL. Carl was a key member of the famous Cactus Air Force and Flying Leathernecks, which ravaged Japan's naval air and army air forces during the campaign for the Solomon Islands in the Pacific during World War II. He became the Marine Corps' first ace in the war, amassing a kill total of 18.5 aerial victories over Japanese aircraft. After the war, Carl became a test pilot at Pax River's Naval Air Test Center (NATC) and was highly respected in the test-piloting realm. He was the Marine Corps' first helicopter pilot and later flew combat missions in various rotorcraft and aircraft in the Vietnam War. (US Marine Corps.)

US Naval Legend. Rear Adm. John Sidney "Slew" McCain (right), grandfather of US senator John McCain, speaks with an unidentified officer at the commissioning ceremony for NAS Pax River on April 1, 1943. McCain served as chief of air operations at NAS Pax River and was a prominent figure in US naval history. In 1942, John S. McCain served as commander of all air forces operating from land bases during the Battle of Guadalcanal. From 1944 to 1945, he served as commander of the US Fast Carrier Task Force in the Pacific. Through his superb leadership in this role, the Navy was able to achieve victories in the battles for the Philippines and Okinawa and helped bring about a successful conclusion to the war against Japan. Sadly, he passed away four days following Japan's formal surrender at a ceremony aboard the battleship USS *Missouri*, anchored in Tokyo Bay. (US National Archives, Still Pictures Branch.)

Officially Open for Business. The commissioning ceremony for NAS Patuxent River took place on April 1, 1943. In the photograph at left are, from left to right, Rear Adm. Ferdinand L. Reichmuth, commandant of Potomac River Naval Command; an unidentified officer; and William T. Rassieur, first commanding officer of NAS Patuxent River. In the photograph at right, Commander Rassieur makes his commissioning ceremony speech. Rear Adm. John S. McCain is seated third from right. (US National Archives, Still Pictures Branch.)

NAVAL BRASS INSPECTION. Rear Adm. John W. Reeves (USN) inspects Squadron VR-9 at NAS Pax River on April 21, 1943. Note the VR-9 Consolidated PBY-5A Catalina parked in the hangar in the left background. (US National Archives, Still Pictures Branch.)

FIRST HANGAR AND AIRCRAFT AT PAX. The first hangar, complete with mast flying a windsock, and an SNJ-3 trainer are seen at NAS Pax River on May 17, 1943. This SNJ-3 trainer was the first aircraft based at the naval air station. (US National Archives, Still Pictures Branch.)

WILDCAT ON FLOATS. This rare Grumman F4F-3 on floats was flight-tested and evaluated at NAS Pax River on May 23, 1943. (US National Archives, Still Pictures Branch.)

CONSTRUCTION OF FIRST FLIGHT TEST HANGAR. Shown here is construction of Hangar I-D at NAS Pax River on July 31, 1943. (US National Archives, Still Pictures Branch.)

AFTER STRAFING, ONE 1000 POUND PRACTICE BOMB DROPPED FROM
F6F-3 DURING SLIGHT GLIDE TO SHOW RICOCHET CHARACTERISTICS.
SPEED - 290 knots.
ALTITUDE - 100 feet.
Target - 12 feet high.

Bomb Ricocheting.

SKIP-BOMBING DEMONSTRATION. On this run, the effectiveness of the skip-bombing technique was successfully demonstrated when a 1,000-pound practice bomb was dropped from the F6F-3 Hellcat flight-test aircraft. The bomb ricocheted off the water and struck the 12-foot-high target on land at the shore of the Patuxent River. Pax River test pilots found that the most effective results were produced in horizontal flight, as opposed to the glide-bombing method. The successful Pax River skip-bombing tests, conducted in August 1943, led the Navy and the Army Air Forces to adopt this low-altitude tactic when attacking Japanese ships and shore installations in the Pacific. As a result, significant damage was caused to the Japanese naval and shipping fleets as well as shore installations throughout the numerous Pacific islands held by Japan. (US National Archives, Textual Reference Branch.)

CORSAIR READIED FOR SKIP-BOMBING DEMONSTRATION. A 1,000-pound, water-filled practice bomb is mounted on the centerline underside fuselage rack of a Vought F4U-1 Corsair flight-test aircraft. The plane took part in skip-bombing demonstration flight tests. (US National Archives, Textual Reference Branch.)

F6F-3 HELLCAT FLIGHT-TEST AIRCRAFT. This is a front view of the Grumman F6F-3 flight-test aircraft. The plane is loaded with water-filled practice bombs for skip-bombing demonstration flights in August 1943. (US National Archives, Textual Reference Branch.)

F6F-3 HELLCAT, SIDE VIEW. The F6F-3 flight-test aircraft is seen here following skip-bombing demonstration flights in August 1943. The Hellcat proved to be a powerful and rugged combat aircraft for the Navy in the Pacific skies during World War II, racking up an impressive aerial kill total that surpassed that of its formidable Pacific partner, the Chance Vought F4U Corsair. (US National Archives, Textual Reference Branch.)

NAVAL AIR STATION EXPANSION. This aerial photograph of NAS Pax River in August 1943 shows evidence of rapid expansion at the facility. Administration offices are visible to the left of center; at right are numerous tents and barracks for naval air station construction crews. The Seaplane Hangar and Basin are visible at the upper right. (US National Archives, Still Pictures Branch.)

ADVANCED AVENGER PROTOTYPE. A Grumman XTBF-3 advanced Avenger torpedo bomber prototype awaits flight- and carrier-suitability trials at NAS Pax River on November 26, 1943. (US National Archives, Still Pictures Branch.)

PAX RIVER FLIGHT-TEST FACILITIES. This is an early view of the Flight-Test Hangar (right background), Electronics Test (center), and Armament Test (left of center) facilities at NAS Pax River. The northwest-facing view in this photograph was taken on December 6, 1943. (US National Archives, Still Pictures Branch.)

NAVALIZED SPITFIRE. Shown here is a British Royal Navy Fleet Air Arm (FAA) Supermarine Seafire at NAS Pax River on December 9, 1943. The navalized Spitfire was test-flown and evaluated, including undergoing carrier-feasibility testing, by Pax River test pilots. Constructive comments and aircraft design and performance data were provided to the British that helped improve the operational performance of the aircraft. (US National Archives, Still Pictures Branch.)

XPB2M-1R Mars Transport Prototype. The gigantic Martin XPB2M-1R Mars transport prototype taxis into NAS Patuxent River after landing on the Patuxent River on December 10, 1943. (US National Archives, Still Pictures Branch.)

Loading Up the Martin Mars. The anchored Martin Mars Navy flying boat transport is loaded with cargo and supplies transported by boat to the aircraft in the Patuxent River on December 11, 1943. The aircraft was being loaded for a supply mission to Natal, Brazil, a flight covering approximately 4,375 miles (an Allied wartime record), on January 24, 1944. (US National Archives, Still Pictures Branch.)

MARTIN MARS TAXIS ONTO THE PATUXENT RIVER. The huge Martin Mars taxis onto the Patuxent River in preparation for takeoff on a wartime record-setting supply mission to Natal, Brazil, on January 24, 1944. (US National Archives, Still Pictures Branch.)

ADVANCED CORONADO FLYING BOAT PROTOTYPE. This is a front view of the hulking Consolidated XPB2Y-4 Coronado prototype, beached at Pax River, on December 27, 1943. The aircraft was at Pax River for fleet-acceptance trials. This Coronado prototype featured four powerful Wright R-2600 radial engines, significantly enhancing the aircraft's performance over previous versions of the gigantic flying boat. The Coronado performed bombing and antisubmarine warfare (ASW) sorties in the Pacific during World War II. (US National Archives, Still Pictures Branch.)

ADVANCED ROYAL NAVY DIVE/TORPEDO BOMBER. This Royal Navy Fleet Air Arm (FAA) Fairey Barracuda dive/torpedo bomber underwent carrier-suitability trials and general flight-testing at Pax River on January 7, 1944. This was the Royal Navy's first all-metal aircraft design and appeared late in World War II. Royal Navy Barracudas, operating from British carriers, caused considerable damage to the German battleship *Tirpitz* in dive-bombing attacks carried out in April, July, and August 1944. (US National Archives, Still Pictures Branch.)

DEEP-SEA DIVER TO THE RESCUE. A Navy deep-sea diver commences a salvage operation dive in the Patuxent River on January 13, 1944. (US National Archives, Still Pictures Branch.)

GOODYEAR FG-1 CORSAIR TURBOJET TESTBED. A Pax River NATC test pilot prepares to take off on a turbojet technology operations familiarization test flight in a Goodyear FG-1 Corsair turbojet testbed on January 18, 1944. (US National Archives, Still Pictures Branch.)

PREPARING TO FLIGHT-TEST AMERICA'S FIRST JET. An Army Bell P-59 Airacomet is wheeled out of the Flight Test Hangar at NAS Pax River for testing on January 20, 1944. This aircraft was later converted to a navalized version, complete with a Navy tricolor scheme, and redesignated as a YP-59A. The aircraft was provided to the Navy by the Army for flight-testing and carrier-feasibility trials. (US National Archives, Still Pictures Branch.)

AIRACOMET IN FLIGHT. A Bell YP-59A, America's first jet aircraft, is in flight. (US National Archives, Still Pictures Branch.)

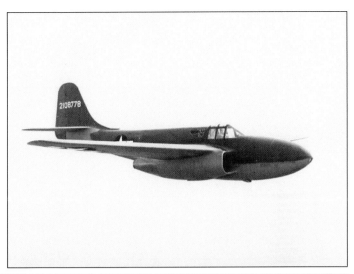

CARRIER DECK TURNTABLE LANDING PLATFORM. This turntable landing platform, complete with arresting wires, was used by Pax River flight-test personnel to evaluate carrier-suitability characteristics of aircraft. This was not the first turntable landing platform to be used by the US Navy; a similar device was used to conduct carrier-feasibility tests at NAS Hampton Roads, Virginia, (now NAS Norfolk, Virginia) in 1921 for aircraft operating aboard the nation's first aircraft carrier, the USS *Langley*. This photograph was taken on January 20, 1944. The turntable landing platform was located in the southwestern portion of the naval air station. (US National Archives, Still Pictures Branch.)

Test Pilot Aaron Storrs and Lt. Comdr. Joel Gayler. Pax River jet test pilot Aaron P. Storrs (right) and Lt. Comdr. Joel Gayler inspect the cockpit of a Bell P-59 Airacomet at Pax River in late January 1944. Storrs became the commanding officer of NAS Patuxent River in late 1944. (US National Archives, Still Pictures Branch.)

Airacomet Flight-Trial Takeoff. This blended image shows test pilot Aaron P. Storrs piloting a Bell P-59 Airacomet on a flight-trial takeoff at NAS Pax River in late January 1944. (US National Archives, Still Pictures Branch.)

Airacomet on Landing Approach. Test pilot Aaron P. Storrs brings a P-59 Airacomet into a perfect landing at NAS Pax River in late January 1944. (US National Archives, Still Pictures Branch.)

Seaplane Basin and Squadron VR-8 Hangar. Shown here on January 20, 1944, are the Seaplane Basin and Squadron VR-8 Hangar at NAS Pax River. Note the VR-8 Consolidated PBY-5A Catalina flying boat to the left of the hangar and the VR-8 Martin PBM Mariner flying boat to the upper right of the hangar. (US National Archives, Still Pictures Branch.)

PROTOTYPE "ASSAULT DRONE." An Interstate Aircraft and Engineering Corporation XTD3R-1 Prototype "Assault Drone" awaits flight trials on March 18, 1944. Production versions of this prototype, designated as TDR-1s, carried torpedoes or bombs and were used by the Navy to attack high-priority/high-risk (to American aircrews) Japanese targets in the Pacific with great success. (US National Archives, Still Pictures Branch.)

"ASSAULT DRONE" BOMB CARRIER. An Interstate Aircraft and Engineering Corporation TDR-1 production version "Assault Drone," carrying bombs, awaits fleet-suitability and weapons-testing trials at NAS Pax River on March 18, 1944. Between September 27, 1944, and October 27, 1944, Special Task Air Group 1 TDR-1s, remotely controlled from TBM Avenger aircraft and carrying bombs, successfully attacked Japanese ships and troop emplacements on islands in the South Pacific. (US National Archives, Still Pictures Branch.)

"ASSAULT DRONE" TORPEDO CARRIER. Seen here on March 21, 1944, is an Interstate Aircraft and Engineering Corporation TDR-1 production version "Assault Drone." The plane, carrying a torpedo, awaits fleet-suitability and weapons-testing trials at NAS Pax River. Special Task Air Group 1 TDR-1s, remotely controlled from TBM Avenger aircraft and carrying torpedoes, attacked Japanese ships in the South Pacific between September 27, 1944, and October 27, 1944. (US National Archives, Still Pictures Branch.)

SECRETARY OF THE NAVY'S PERSONAL AIRCRAFT. Secretary of the Navy Frank Knox's personal R5D-1 military transport aircraft is shown in flight over Pax River on March 21, 1944. (US National Archives, Still Pictures Branch.)

REICH DEFENDER. In May 1944, this captured German Focke Wulf Fw-190 A-4 was flight-tested and evaluated at NAS Pax River. The aircraft held its own when flown in simulated aerial combat with top-line Navy fighters, but it did not possess as much firepower. The Fw-190, however, proved to be one of the finest German propeller-driven fighters of World War II, causing considerable damage to massive Army Air Forces bomber formations that pounded the Third Reich by day. Together with the Messerschmitt Me-109 Gustav, the "Butcher Bird," as the Fw-190 was nicknamed, formed the backbone of the Luftwaffe's daylight fighter force. (US National Archives, Still Pictures Branch.)

MARINE CORPS MITCHELL. A Marine Corps North American PBJ-1J patrol bomber is on a test flight over Pax River on May 29, 1944. The PBJ was used by the Navy and Marine Corps in the Pacific during the latter portion of World War II. This plane caused great damage to Japanese shipping and air bases in the Pacific. (US National Archives, Still Pictures Branch.)

RAF Bomber Command Mainstay. In 1944, this RAF Bomber Command Avro Lancaster Mk. III heavy bomber paid a visit to NAS Pax River. British Lancasters formed the backbone of the RAF's Bomber Command heavy-bomber force and were best known for their devastating incendiary night raids on the German cities of Dresden, Hamburg, and Cologne. (US National Archives, Still Pictures Branch.)

Royal Navy Fleet Air Arm (FAA) Fairey Firefly. A British Royal Navy FAA Fairey Firefly fighter is shown under evaluation at NAS Pax River. (US National Archives, Still Pictures Branch.)

CONESTOGA IN FLIGHT. A Navy Budd RB-1 Conestoga transport is seen in flight above NAS Pax River on June 3, 1944. The stainless-steel airplane ushered in new design specifics that are now common in military cargo aircraft. The plane had several of the same features found in the German Junkers Ju-90 and Ju-290 military transports, most notably the cargo ramp at the rear of the airplane. (US National Archives, Still Pictures Branch.)

CURTISS SB2C-3 HELLDIVER. Shown here awaiting flight-testing on June 5, 1944, is a Navy Curtiss SB2C-3 Helldiver dive-bomber. The SB2C-3 was an early version of the Helldiver. The Helldiver was developed as a replacement for the aging and venerable Douglas SBD ("Slow But Deadly") Dauntless dive-bomber that achieved fame during the Battle of Midway. (US National Archives, Still Pictures Branch.)

PRIVATEER PROTOTYPE. The Navy Consolidated-Vultee XPB4Y-2 Privateer long-range patrol bomber prototype awaits flight trials at NAS Pax River on June 6, 1944. This photograph was taken on D-day, the Allied invasion of Normandy, France. The Privateer was later deployed on combat duty half a world away, in the Pacific. The plane, bristling with defensive armament, wreaked devastation on Japanese naval shipping and naval air forces. (US National Archives, Still Pictures Branch.)

"WHISTLING DEATH." A gull-winged Navy Chance Vought F4U-1D Corsair is being prepared for flight-testing at NAS Pax River in early June 1944. The Corsair underwent fleet-suitability flight trials and, when introduced into combat in the Pacific, was appropriately nicknamed "Whistling Death" by the Japanese. The aircraft was one of the finest fighters to see combat in World War II; together with the Grumman Hellcat, it ravaged Japanese naval and army air forces in the Pacific. (US National Archives, Textual Reference Branch.)

MARINER TRANSPORT. A VR-8 Martin PBM Mariner flying boat transport is shown in flight, departing NAS Pax River on June 20, 1944. (US National Archives, Still Pictures Branch.)

WICKED PRIVATEER. A production-version Consolidated-Vultee PB4Y-2 Privateer long-range patrol bomber awaits fleet-suitability flight trials at NAS Pax River on June 30, 1944. The aircraft participated in tactical flight evaluation fly-offs with Navy flying boats also used for patrol duty. The Privateer emerged as the clear winner in the performance and firepower categories. (US National Archives, Still Pictures Branch.)

PBJ with a Big Gun. This is a close-up view of the nose of a North American PBJ-1, outfitted with a 75-millimeter cannon. The aircraft was flight-tested and evaluated at NAS Pax River during World War II. Evaluators discovered, through the flight tests, that the cannon-equipped PBJ-1 could be a devastating weapon against shipping, surfaced submarines, and land targets. As a result of the flight tests, the Army was persuaded to equip its B-25H Mitchell bombers with 75-millimeter cannons as well. The Marine Corps and Navy acquired Army B-25Hs for outfitting with those cannons; together with Army B-25Hs, these planes caused tremendous damage to Japanese shipping, naval targets, and land targets. (US National Archives, Textual Reference Branch.)

Radar-Equipped Avenger. An ASD wingtip, radar-equipped General Motors TBM-1D Avenger torpedo bomber awaits fleet suitability flight trials at NAS Pax River on July 4, 1944. The ASD radar was used in strike missions against Japanese shipping and naval warships to great effect, contributing to numerous successful attacks on Japanese vessels during the latter part of World War II. (US National Archives, Textual Reference Branch.)

WORLD WAR II TRAINING MAINSTAY. A North American SNJ-3 trainer, a US Navy training mainstay during the war, is seen at NAS Pax River on July 11, 1944. (US National Archives, Still Pictures Branch.)

RADAR-EQUIPPED DAUNTLESS. A Douglas SBD-5 Dauntless dive-bomber, equipped with an APS-4 anti-shipping radar unit mounted on an underwing bomb rack, awaits fleet-suitability trials on July 13, 1944. The Dauntless was affectionately called "Slow But Deadly" by its aircrews. By this stage of World War II, this was the Navy's and Marine Corps's aging and veteran dive-bomber. It achieved fame at the Battle of Midway in early June 1942, when Navy SBD-3s from aircraft carriers sent four Japanese aircraft carriers to the bottom of the Pacific Ocean, delivering a major blow to the Imperial Japanese Navy and turning the tide of the war in the Pacific. (US National Archives, Still Pictures Branch.)

RADAR-EQUIPPED HELLDIVER. A Curtiss SB2C-3 Helldiver dive-bomber, equipped with an APS-4 anti-shipping radar unit mounted on an underwing bomb rack, awaits fleet-suitability flight trials at NAS Pax River on July 13, 1944. The Helldiver was developed as a replacement for the aging Douglas SBD Dauntless dive-bomber. (US National Archives, Still Pictures Branch.)

BENT-WINGED SCOUT. The Douglas XBTD-6 scout torpedo bomber prototype is shown here undergoing flight trials above NAS Pax River on July 20, 1944. (US National Archives, Still Pictures Branch.)

CURTISS SC-1 SEAHAWK. Shown during takeoff from the Patuxent River on a flight trial is a Curtiss SC-1 Seahawk scout seaplane. Note the pilot giving a thumbs-up, indicating satisfactory takeoff performance of the aircraft. This photograph was taken on August 5, 1944. (US National Archives, Still Pictures Branch.)

TIGERCAT PERFORMING FLIGHT TRIALS. A Grumman F7F-2 Tigercat is shown on a fleet-suitability test flight above NAS Pax River on September 1, 1944. The Tigercat was the Navy's first twin-engined fighter. Although the airplane was too big for carrier operations, it became operational with the Marine Corps during World War II. However, it never saw combat during the war. (US National Archives, Still Pictures Branch.)

ADVANCED ZERO UNDERGOING FLIGHT EVALUATION. On September 25, 1944, this captured Imperial Japanese Naval Air Force Mitsubishi A6M5 Type 52 Zero was flight-tested and evaluated in the skies above NAS Pax River. The Type 52 Zero had a more powerful engine than earlier versions of the Zero, as well as improved firepower, in the form of cannons in the wings. However, the aircraft suffered from the same deficiencies as its predecessors: inadequate armor protection for the pilot and a lack of self-sealing fuel tanks. In essence, the Zero sacrificed these elements for speed and exceptional maneuverability. (US National Archives, Still Pictures Branch.)

JOINT ARMY-NAVY FIGHTER CONFERENCE. The flight line at the Joint Army-Navy Fighter Conference at NAS Pax River is shown on October 17, 1944. Note the British Royal Navy Seafire (a navalized version of the famous Spitfire) at the upper left. The Joint Fighter Conference was held October 16–23, 1944, at Pax River. At this conference, US Army, US Navy, RAF/Royal Navy, National Advisory Committee for Aeronautics (NACA), and US fighter aircraft industry test pilots were afforded the opportunity to fly and evaluate a variety of US and foreign fighter aircraft, including captured Axis aircraft, and freely exchange information and comments regarding the performance of these aircraft. Among the test pilots present were NACA Langley Memorial Aeronautical Laboratory (LMAL) engineering test pilots Mel Gough and Herb Hoover. (US National Archives, Still Pictures Branch.)

ARMY AIR FORCES BLACK WIDOW. A US Army Air Forces Northrop P-61A Black Widow night fighter sits on the flight line at NAS Pax River during the Joint Army-Navy Fighter Conference on October 19, 1944. The Black Widow was one of the finest night fighters to see combat during World War II. (US National Archives, Still Pictures Branch.)

AIRCRAFT COMPANY REPRESENTATIVES. Chance Vought personnel pose beside one of the company's F4U-1D Corsairs at the Joint Fighter Conference on October 18, 1944. Shown here are, from left to right, W.L. Lowe, F. Taylor, A.L. Brill, J.B. Schllemann, W. Horan, W.H. McCarthy, I.N. Palley, Paul Baker, and J.R. Clark. Pilot Ben Towle is seated in the cockpit, and N. Siegle is standing on the wing. (US National Archives, Still Pictures Branch.)

JOINT FIGHTER CONFERENCE CHAIRMAN. Comdr. P.H. Ramsey (USN), Joint Fighter Conference chairman, boards a Republic P-47M prior to embarking on a familiarization flight at the conference at NAS Pax River on October 16, 1944. (US National Archives, Still Pictures Branch.)

BELL TEST PILOT JACK WOOLAMS. On October 18, 1944, test pilot Jack Woolams radios the tower before taking off in a British Royal Navy Firefly during the Joint Fighter Conference at NAS Pax River. (US National Archives, Still Pictures Branch.)

PARTICIPANTS AT JOINT FIGHTER Conference. Officials attending the Joint Fighter Conference on October 16, 1944, are, from left to right, Comdr. T.D. Tyre (USN), VF Design Bureau of Aeronautics Air Committee; Capt. N.R. Buckle (RAF); T.C. Lonnquest (USN), director of the Engineering Division of the Bureau of Aeronautics; and Col. R.S. Gorman (AAF), Air Technical Services Command (ATSC), Wright Field. (US National Archives, Still Pictures Branch.)

MITSUBISHI A6M5 TYPE 52 ZERO. A captured Japanese Mitsubishi A6M5 Type 52 Zero (a late-war version of the Type 21 Zero) is under evaluation at NAS Pax River during the Joint Fighter Conference on October 21, 1944. The aircraft featured an improved engine as well as increased firepower: two cannons rather than machine guns in the wings. (US National Archives, Still Pictures Branch.)

BUBBLE-TOP CANOPY CORSAIR. A Goodyear FG-1 Corsair awaits flight trials and fleet-suitability tests at NAS Pax River on October 31, 1944. The FG-1 featured a bubble-top or teardrop canopy for enhanced vision for the pilot. (US National Archives, Textual Reference Branch.)

AMERICA'S FIRST HELICOPTER. The Sikorsky HNS-1 Hoverfly, America's first practical helicopter, awaits flight trials and fleet-suitability testing in a flight-test hangar in late 1944. Army HNS-1s, designated as YR4Bs, were deployed to combat theaters in the Pacific toward the end of World War II, successfully retrieving downed Allied pilots and aircrews in Search and Rescue (SAR) missions. (US National Archives, Textual Reference Branch.)

SIKORSKY HNS-1 ON FLOATS. This Sikorsky HNS-1 Hoverfly was outfitted with floats and flight-tested to determine the feasibility of water operations with rotorcraft on November 2, 1944. (US National Archives, Textual Reference Branch.)

BRITISH ROYAL NAVY SEAFIRE. An advanced Royal Navy Supermarine Seafire awaits flight trials and carrier-suitability trials at NAS Pax River on December 13, 1944. (US National Archives, Still Pictures Branch.)

ADVANCED GOODYEAR FG-1 CORSAIR. A Goodyear XF2G-1 Corsair prototype awaits flight trials at NAS Pax River on February 2, 1945. (US National Archives, Still Pictures Branch.)

CORSAIR PROTOTYPE. A late-war Chance Vought XF4U-4 Corsair prototype is seen here before undergoing flight trials and fleet-suitability trials on March 1, 1945. (US National Archives, Still Pictures Branch.)

HELLDIVER FEASIBILITY FLIGHT TESTS. A late-war Curtiss SB2C-4 Helldiver awaits dive/torpedo bomber feasibility flight tests on March 16, 1945. Naval planners, interested in seeing if the Helldiver could relieve overworked Avenger carrier-based bomber squadrons, requested that Pax River perform this important trial. For the test, the Helldiver carried a torpedo in the bomb bay; this necessitated that the bomb bay doors be kept open. The test results showed that too much drag was caused by the addition of the torpedo, making the aircraft much slower. Therefore, US naval brass decided that the Helldiver should be used strictly as a dive-bomber. Torpedo-carrying flight tests were also performed at Pax River with Grumman F6F Hellcats and Lockheed PV-1 Venturas, which were found to be adequate torpedo carriers. (US National Archives, Textual Reference Branch.)

LATE-WAR HELLCAT. A Grumman F6F-5 Hellcat loaded up with bombs and a drop tank is shown before undergoing a weapons-carrying and ground attack flight-test demonstration at NAS Pax River on March 27, 1945. (US National Archives, Still Pictures Branch.)

MITSUBISHI KI-46 DINAH. A captured Imperial Japanese Army Air Force Mitsubishi Ki-46 Dinah high-speed reconnaissance aircraft undergoes flight evaluation over NAS Pax River on March 29, 1945. The Dinah was also used by the Japanese as an interceptor against high-flying Army Air Forces Boeing B-29 Superfortress formations devastating the Japanese mainland. The interceptor Dinah variants were equipped with oblique upward-firing cannons for flying beneath the US heavy bombers and firing the cannon salvos into the bomb bays of the bombers. This tactic proved to be successful in some instances, incinerating the large bombers in the air. This particular Dinah was provided to Pax River by the Technical Air Intelligence Center (TAIC) at NAS Anacostia, DC. (US National Archives, Still Pictures Branch.)

NAKAJIMA B5N2 KATE FLIGHT EVALUATION. A captured Imperial Japanese Naval Air Force (IJNAF) Nakajima B5N2 Kate (late-war version) undergoes flight evaluation at NAS Pax River on April 26, 1945. The Kate was one of the best torpedo bombers of World War II, leading numerous successful torpedo and bombing missions against US forces in the Pacific. (US National Archives, Textual Reference Branch.)

GRUMMAN F7F-3N TIGERCAT NIGHT FIGHTER. A Grumman F7F-3N Tigercat night fighter awaits flight- and fleet-suitability trials on June 1, 1945. In spring 1945, Bell Laboratories sought to test its latest invention, the SCR 720-A scanning radar. This system was installed in the Grumman F7F-3N and flight-tested at Pax River. The radar system and the aircraft were found to be "superior" to other night fighters and their radar systems in service at the time. The Tigercat night fighter was deployed to Marine Corps combat units in the Pacific during the last couple of months of World War II, but it never saw combat before the war ended in September 1945. The F7F-3N, used by the Marine Corps in combat during the Korean War, experienced marked success in that conflict, downing several North Korean Polikarpov Po-2 "Bedcheck Charlie" biplanes that harassed US and United Nations (UN) forces at night by dropping bombs on military installations and troop emplacements. (US National Archives, Textual Reference Branch.)

PBJ-1 WITH SIMULATED BATTLE DAMAGE. A radar-equipped North American PBJ-1, with shortened radar nacelle to simulate flak damage, is seen before undergoing flight-testing at NAS Pax River on June 4, 1945. Given the aircraft's design, concerns were raised about the potential for aerodynamic problems in the event it sustained flak damage to the wingtip radar system. Hence, the need for flight-testing, which revealed that no aerodynamic problems would be experienced in the event of such damage to the airplane while in flight. As a result, radar-equipped PBJ-1s were deployed, with confidence, in combat toward the end of World War II. (US National Archives, Textual Reference Branch.)

FULLY INTACT PBJ-1. A radar-equipped North American PBJ-1, with intact radar nacelle, undergoes flight-testing at NAS Pax River on June 4, 1945. (US National Archives, Textual Reference Branch.)

IMPERIAL JAPANESE ARMY AIR FORCE (IJAAF) KI-61 HIEN "TONY" FIGHTER. A Naval Air Test Center (NATC) pilot performs a test flight in a captured IJAAF Kawasaki Ki-61 "Tony" fighter over NAS Pax River on June 23, 1945. In the hands of an experienced pilot, the "Tony" proved to be a match for excellent American fighters, such as the North American P-51 Mustang. (US National Archives, Still Pictures Branch.)

Prop/Jet Fighter Flight Trials. A Ryan FR-1 Fireball undergoes flight trials in late June 1945. The aircraft is being powered by a turbojet at the rear of the aircraft, while the prop is feathered. (US National Archives, Still Pictures Branch.)

Lockheed P-80A Shooting Star. A Lockheed P-80A Shooting Star jet fighter awaits carrier suitability flight-testing at NAS Pax River on August 1, 1945. The carrier-suitability tests of the Shooting Star revealed that the aircraft was ill suited for carrier operations. (US National Archives, Textual Reference Branch.)

PBY-5A Catalina Flying Boat. A late-war Consolidated PBY-5A Catalina flying boat is ready for flight trials on August 9, 1945, the day the United States dropped the second atomic bomb on Japan—specifically, the city of Nagasaki. The strategic move effectively forced a Japanese surrender and an end to World War II. Note the Sikorsky HNS-1 Hoverfly helicopter on floats in the background right of center. A Curtiss SC-1 Seahawk is in the background at far right. (US National Archives, Textual Reference Branch.)

Simulated High-Altitude Testing. Volunteers participate in simulated high-altitude human-factors testing in the Low-Pressure Chamber at NAS Pax River on August 18, 1945. The two female volunteers worked in the naval air station's pharmacy. (US National Archives, Still Pictures Branch.)

GERMAN FLYING BOAT. A captured German Blohm & Voss BV 222 Wiking ("Viking") flying boat in British markings sits at Ila Fjord in Trondheim, Norway, on August 27, 1945. The Wiking was the largest flying boat to see combat during World War II. This particular aircraft was flown to England, where it was test-flown by Capt. Eric Brown, a famous Royal Navy test pilot. NAS Pax River obtained a similar aircraft and test-flew it at the naval air station. Important design data was obtained from these flight tests and was ultimately incorporated in the hull design of the Convair R3Y Tradewind flying boat, which became fleet operational with the Navy in the 1950s. (US National Archives, Still Pictures Branch.)

GRUMMAN BEARCAT. A Grumman F8F-1C Bearcat is shown before undergoing flight trials at NAS Pax River on September 28, 1945. An evaluation of the aircraft's 20-millimeter cannons in the wings was conducted during the trials. World War II ended before the Bearcat became fleet operational with the US Navy and Marine Corps. (US National Archives, Textual Reference Branch.)

AERODYNAMIC ARROW. A captured German Dornier Do-335A Pfeil ("Arrow") is under evaluation at the Naval Air Test Center (NATC) at NAS Pax River on November 3, 1945. The Do-335 served as a fighter-bomber and featured a unique push-pull powerplant configuration with a propeller located in both the nose and the tail. The aircraft was capable of speeds up to 475 miles per hour, making it the fastest piston-engined aircraft of World War II. (US National Archives, Still Pictures Branch.)

SUPERB SCHWALBE ("SWALLOW"). In October 1945, the NATC at Pax River acquired three captured German Messerschmitt Me-262 Schwalbe ("Swallow") jet fighters for flight-testing and evaluation. The Schwalbe was the world's first combat operational jet fighter and, had it been produced in greater numbers and introduced into combat earlier in the war, would have been a game changer affecting the course of World War II. Flight evaluations of the Me-262, including the one shown here, yielded important design and data for high-performance jet fighters with slight wing sweep. This data was incorporated in the design characteristics of numerous US military jet fighters and bombers. The aircraft in this photograph, taken in February 1946, was nicknamed "Screamin' Meemie" by Navy evaluators. The plane was test-flown for a total of 10.2 hours at NAS Pax River. (US National Archives, Textual Reference Branch.)

ARADO AR-234 B-2 BLITZ JET BOMBER. In March 1946, this captured German Arado Ar-234 B-2 Blitz, the world's first combat operational jet bomber, was static-evaluated at NAS Pax River. The aircraft had been flight-evaluated during a one-hour ferry flight from Newark, New Jersey, to Pax River. The aircraft possessed good flight qualities, but evaluators found the cockpit layout unimpressive. The aircraft was nicknamed "Jane I" by Navy and Marine Corps evaluators. (US National Archives, Textual Reference Branch.)

JUNKERS JUMO 004 ENGINE. The key to the success of the Messerschmitt Me-262 and Arado 234 jet aircraft was the revolutionary Junkers Jumo 004 turbo-jet engine. Here, one such engine is being evaluated in a lab at NAS Pax River. (US National Archives, Textual Reference Branch.)

H8K2 EMILY FLYING BOAT ON THE RIVER. A captured IJNAF Kawanishi H8K2 Emily flying boat taxis along the Patuxent River after completing a flight test at NAS Pax River on August 20, 1946. (US National Archives, Still Pictures Branch.)

H8K2 EMILY FLYING BOAT ON THE TARMAC. The captured IJNAF Kawanishi H8K2 Emily flying boat is beached on the tarmac at the Seaplane Basin at NAS Pax River on February 18, 1947. (US National Archives, Still Pictures Branch.)

Three

THE US NAVY ENTERS THE JET AGE AND THE ALLIED EFFORT IN KOREA
1946–1960

Following World War II, the US Navy commenced flight-testing and evaluation of America's first carrier-based, high-performance jet aircraft and specialized, prop-driven aircraft at the Naval Air Test Center (NATC) at NAS Patuxent River. This function became critical to the nation keeping up with rapid advancements in jet and post–World War II prop technology by the Soviet Union, America's new threat to national security. The outbreak of the Korean War on June 25, 1950, and rising tensions related to the Cold War spurred the furious development of advanced aircraft technologies and radical new aircraft concepts in the United States.

It was a boom time for the American aircraft industry, as new aircraft and aircraft weapons systems production surpassed levels achieved during World War II. The jet age was still in its infancy, but its potential was quickly becoming realized. The NATC at NAS Pax River was ideally suited to perform critical flight-testing and carrier-adaptability testing of high-performance jets. After World War II, NATC's primary function became the conduction of carrier-suitability and service-acceptance trials of all US naval aircraft.

With the advent of the jet age came the routine use of air-to-air missiles in combat. Pax River played a crucial role in the flight-testing of these weapons, which were launched from aircraft in trial and target tests.

Advanced rotorcraft were developed for the Navy and Marine Corps after World War II. Feasibility and carrier-suitability flight-testing of these whirlybirds was performed at Pax River. After World War II, in late 1945, the United States Naval Test Pilot School (USNTPS) was established at NAS Patuxent River to enable test pilots to become proficient in the art of operating advanced US naval aircraft. Several graduates of the USNTPS and NATC veterans would later be selected by the National Aeronautics and Space Administration (NASA) to serve as astronauts and perform critical roles in America's highly successful and productive manned space programs.

GOODYEAR XF2G-1 CORSAIR PROTOTYPE. An early post–World War II Goodyear XF2G-1 Corsair prototype awaits flight trials outside the Flight Test Hangar at NAS Pax River. (US National Archives, Still Pictures Branch.)

F6F-5N HELLCAT NIGHT FIGHTER. A Grumman F6F-5N Hellcat night fighter is shown during flight- and fleet-acceptance trials at NAS Pax River in 1946. (US National Archives, Still Pictures Branch.)

MAGNIFICENT MAULER. A Martin XBTM-1 Mauler prototype loaded with external stores—a bomb and two drop tanks—awaits flight trials and weapons testing at NAS Pax River in July 1947. (US National Archives, Still Pictures Branch.)

TOWED GLIDER SNATCH. A Navy Douglas JD-1 performs a towed glider snatch on July 30, 1947. (US National Archives, Still Pictures Branch.)

"THE TRUCULENT TURTLE." Preflight checks are being performed on "The Turtle," a Lockheed P2V-1 Neptune antisubmarine warfare (ASW) patrol bomber. This photograph was taken at NAS Pax River on September 10, 1947. This aircraft set a new world record for the longest un-refueled flight, flying from Perth, Australia, on September 9, and arriving at Columbus, Ohio, on September 11, 1946. "The Turtle" is now on display at the National Naval Aviation Museum in Pensacola, Florida. (US National Archives, Still Pictures Branch.)

"THE TURTLE" PILOT. Comdr. Thomas D. Davies, pilot of "The Truculent Turtle," poses beside his aircraft for a publicity photograph at Pax River on September 10, 1947. (US National Archives, Still Pictures Branch.)

AMERICA'S FIRST CARRIER-BASED JET. Seen here on September 11, 1947, Pax River ground crews perform maintenance on a McDonnell FD-1 Phantom, America's first carrier-based jet, prior to flight trials and fleet-suitability tests. (US National Archives, Still Pictures Branch.)

"FLYING BANANAS" AND CONSOLIDATED PB4Y-2 PRIVATEER. A pair of Piasecki HRP-1 "Flying Banana" helicopters maintain a hover around a Consolidated PB4Y-2 Privateer patrol bomber at NAS Pax River in September 1947. During the early years of the Cold War, US Navy and Soviet Air Force aircraft tangled in combat. On April 8, 1950, four Soviet Lavochken La-11s shot down a US Navy Privateer patrolling the Baltic Sea area. The Privateer's full complement of crew members (10) perished in the confrontation. (US National Archives, Still Pictures Branch.)

Marvelous Mars. A Martin JRM-2 Mars advanced flying boat taxis on the Patuxent River in October 1947. (US National Archives, Still Pictures Branch.)

First Fleet-Operational Jet Fighter. In January 1948, a North American FJ-1 is being gassed up for flight trials and fleet-acceptability tests. The FJ-1 became the US Navy's first fleet-operational jet fighter. (US National Archives, Still Pictures Branch.)

Cutting-Edge Cutlass. A prototype Chance Vought XF7U-1 Cutlass, a swept-wing tailless jet fighter, undergoes flight trials above NAS Pax River on November 11, 1948. The Cutlass, cutting-edge for its time, was developed from captured World War II German advanced jet aircraft design plans. (US National Archives, Still Pictures Branch.)

TPS Student with Douglas AD-1 Skyraider. A TPS student familiarizes himself with a Douglas AD-1 Skyraider in 1948. The Skyraider, designed as a dive/torpedo bomber, was developed toward the end of World War II. It came too late to see combat in the war, but later served as the Navy's primary attack aircraft in the Korean War and early in the Vietnam War. (US National Archives, Still Pictures Branch.)

ADVANCED NAVY TRAINER. A North American XSN2J-1 trainer prototype awaits flight trials and fleet-suitability tests at NATC Pax River in 1948. (US National Archives, Still Pictures Branch.)

ADVANCED PHANTOM. A McDonnell FH-1 Phantom is shown at NATC Pax River on November 16, 1948. The aircraft, undergoing flight trials, is equipped with a drop tank. (US National Archives, Still Pictures Branch.)

CUTLASS PROTOTYPES. On January 4, 1949, two XF7U-1 Cutlass prototypes await flight-testing and evaluation at NAS Pax River. (US National Archives, Still Pictures Branch.)

XF7U-1 CUTLASS PROTOTYPE TEST FLIGHT. Here, an XF7U-1 Cutlass prototype performs a low-altitude test flight over the Patuxent River. (US National Archives, Still Pictures Branch.)

F8F-1 Bearcat Catapult Launch. Prospective TPS student test pilots observe a TPS Grumman F8F-1 Bearcat catapult launch on February 3, 1949. The catapult officer, at far left, gives an "all clear" signal to the pilot for launch. (US National Archives, Still Pictures Branch.)

Douglas R5D-5 Transport. A post–World War II Douglas R5D-5 transport is shown at NAS Pax River on April 15, 1949. (US National Archives, Still Pictures Branch.)

PANTHER PHENOM. In May 1949, Pax River conducted service-acceptance trials of a new fleet defender. This plane, the Grumman F9F-2 Panther, would serve the Navy well during the Korean War. The Panther was Grumman's first jet endeavor. Pioneering astronauts Alan Shepard and John Glenn racked up many hours of flight time in Panther jets at Pax River. The Panther managed to achieve numerous aerial victories over sleek North Korean and Chinese MiG-15 jet fighters. (US National Archives, Still Pictures Branch.)

NAVALIZED SUPERFORTRESS. A Boeing P2-B, a navalized version of the famous Boeing B-29 Superfortress, awaits flight- and fleet-suitability trials at NAS Pax River in October 1949. (US National Archives, Still Pictures Branch.)

KOREAN WAR–ERA DOUGLAS AD-4. A Douglas AD-4 Skyraider performs flight trials above NAS Pax River on October 26, 1949. Several carrier-based Navy A-1E advanced Skyraiders gained the distinction of shooting down two North Vietnamese Air Force Mikoyan-Gurevich MiG-17 Fresco subsonic jet fighters early in the Vietnam War, a testament to the soundness of the Skyraider's aerodynamic design. (US National Archives, Still Pictures Branch.)

RADAR-EQUIPPED SKYRAIDER. A Douglas AD-3W Skyraider, an antisubmarine warfare (ASW) version of the Skyraider, undergoes flight trials above NAS Pax River on November 10, 1949. In addition to being equipped with a large radar bulge on its underside, the aircraft is carrying drop tanks. (US National Archives, Still Pictures Branch.)

GUARDIAN PROTOTYPE. A Grumman XTB3F-1S Guardian prototype is shown undergoing flight- and fleet-suitability trials on December 15, 1949. In addition to having a turbojet in the tail, the aircraft featured an underside radome, enclosing an APS-20 radar system. The plane also possessed Electronic Countermeasures (ECM) capability. The Guardian was the Navy's first carrier-based ASW aircraft to become fleet operational. It was replaced by the Grumman S-2 Tracker in 1955. (US National Archives, Still Pictures Branch.)

SKYKNIGHT PROTOTYPE. The Douglas XF3D-1 Skyknight was the US Navy's first fleet-operational, all-weather, radar-equipped jet night fighter. The aircraft served with the Marine Corps during the Korean War, shooting down several North Korean and Chinese MiG-15s. Here, a Skyknight undergoes flight- and fleet-suitability trials above NAS Pax River on December 30, 1949. (US National Archives, Still Pictures Branch.)

SUPER SAVAGE. In early 1950, NAS Pax River began flight-testing a new multirole attack aircraft, the North American AJ-1 Savage. The Savage was the first Navy aircraft to be powered by two piston engines and a turbojet. The turbojet was located in the rear fuselage. The carrier-based aircraft could carry 10,500 pounds of weapons, including nuclear bombs. The Savage was capable of taking off from aircraft carriers without the assistance of a catapult. At Pax, it was extensively tested for carrier suitability. (US National Archives, Still Pictures Branch.)

NAVALIZED FLYING BOXCAR. A Fairchild R4Q, a navalized version of the C-119 Flying Boxcar, awaits flight- and fleet-suitability trials at NAS Pax River on June 20, 1950. R4Qs were used by the Navy and Marine Corps in a cargo transport role throughout the 1950s. (US National Archives, Still Pictures Branch.)

NAVY JET FIGHTERS. This is an in-flight formation of US Navy jet fighters above NATC Pax River in July 1950. Shown here are, from bottom to top, a Chance Vought F7U-1 Cutlass, a McDonnell F2H-2 Banshee, a Grumman F9F-1 Panther, and a Chance Vought F6U-1 Pirate. (US National Archives, Still Pictures Branch.)

NATC FLIGHT OPERATIONS. A Chance Vought F4U-5 Corsair taxis out for a test flight at NATC Pax River in July 1950. The Flight Operations Building is clearly visible in this photograph. (US National Archives, Still Pictures Branch.)

AJ-1 SAVAGE. A North American AJ-1 Savage taxis into NAS Pax River after completing a flight test in August 1950. (US National Archives, Still Pictures Branch.)

NATC ROTORCRAFT TECHNOLOGY. This is a lineup of NATC rotorcraft outside the NATC flight-test hangars in August 1950. Shown here are, from front to back, Kaman (K-255) experimental helicopter, Bell (HTL) helicopter, Piasecki (HRP-2) "Flying Banana" helicopter, and Piasecki (HJP-1) helicopter. (US National Archives, Still Pictures Branch.)

HIGH-VOLUME NATC FLIGHT-TEST ACTIVITY. In this August 1950 NATC scene, a Chance Vought F7U Cutlass is towed via a "mule," while a Douglas AD Skyraider (right) sits with wings folded and a Douglas AD-3W (far right) is powered up. Meanwhile, a Grumman F8F Bearcat (background) is towed into the flight-test area. A Grumman UF-1 amphibian flying boat can be seen in the back to the right. (US National Archives, Still Pictures Branch.)

BEAUTIFUL BANSHEE. During the late 1940s, Pax River conducted service-acceptance trials of the McDonnell F2H Banshee. The aerodynamic soundness of the Banshee's design was proven in dramatic fashion when NATC test pilot and later NASA astronaut Alan B. Shepard, the first American in space, successfully flew a Banshee under a bridge section of the Chesapeake Bay Bridge-Tunnel. His feat drew the ire of the base commander at Pax River. (US National Archives, Still Pictures Branch.)

CHANCE VOUGHT PIRATE. A Chance Vought F6U-1 Pirate makes a landing approach at NATC Pax River in August 1950. This version of the Pirate was equipped with an afterburner. (US National Archives, Still Pictures Branch.)

NAVALIZED WARNING STAR. The Lockheed PO-1 was a Navy version of the famous Lockheed EC-121 Warning Star and served as an airborne early-warning aircraft for the Navy throughout the 1950s. This PO-1 awaits flight- and fleet-suitability trials at NAS Pax River on August 10, 1950. (US National Archives, Still Pictures Branch.)

MERCATOR ABOVE KITTY HAWK. A Pax River–based Martin P4M-1 Mercator patrol bomber is shown above the birthplace of flight, the Wright Brothers Memorial at Kitty Hawk, North Carolina, in August 1950. (US National Archives, Still Pictures Branch.)

SKYRAIDER WEAPONS DEMONSTRATION. A Douglas AD-2 Skyraider, carrying a torpedo, a pair of 500-pound bombs, and twelve 5-inch rockets, climbs in the skies above Pax River on a weapons flight-test demonstration in September 1950. Navy and Marine Corps Skyraiders served in the Korean War, experiencing dramatic success. On May 2, 1951, Skyraider strike aircraft launched a successful torpedo attack on North Korea's Hwacheon Dam, rendering it useless. (US National Archives, Still Pictures Branch.)

CORSAIR RADAR-EQUIPPED NIGHT FIGHTER. A Chance Vought F4U-5N Corsair radar-equipped night fighter awaits flight- and fleet-suitability trials at NAS Pax River in March 1951. Night fighter Corsairs were used by the Navy in the Korean War with great success. (US National Archives, Still Pictures Branch.)

JET-ASSISTED TAKEOFF HELICOPTER. In a special flight-test experiment, jet-assisted takeoff (JATO) was applied to a Marine Corps Sikorsky HRS-1 helicopter and tried upon takeoff at NAS Pax River on January 5, 1952. Lt. Col. Armond H. Delalio (USMC) served as pilot and Lt. Comdr. Edward A. Arnold (USN) was the copilot. (US National Archives, Still Pictures Branch.)

JATO FLIGHT-TEST SUCCESS. A Marine Corps Sikorsky HRS-1 helicopter, operating via JATO, climbs high into the sky above NAS Pax River on January 5, 1952, experiencing apparent initial success. (US National Archives, Still Pictures Branch.)

FLIGHT-TEST CRASH WRECKAGE. Shown here is helicopter debris from a HRS-1 JATO flight-test failure at NAS Pax River on January 5, 1952. In honor of the pilot and copilot who died in the crash, roadways at NAS Pax River were formally dedicated and designated as Delalio Road and Arnold Circle, respectively. (US National Archives, Still Pictures Branch.)

TAILLESS FLEET DEFENDER. Chance Vought used German World War II secret aircraft design data to develop an advanced tailless jet fighter for the Navy. This tailless wonder became known as the F7U-1 Cutlass. The F7U-1 design, however, was in need of beefing up, resulting in the development of the F7U-3 (pictured). The F7U-3 Cutlass served as a fleet defender with the Navy from 1954 to 1957. (US National Archives, Still Pictures Branch.)

GRUMMAN F9F-6 COUGAR. A Grumman F9F-6 Cougar, a swept-wing version of the Grumman F9F-2 Panther, is seen here before flight- and fleet-suitability trials at NAS Pax River in August 1952. (US National Archives, Still Pictures Branch.)

LOCKHEED PO1-W CREW. A Lockheed PO1-W Warning Star crew exits the aircraft at NAS Pax River on September 3, 1952. (US National Archives, Still Pictures Branch.)

MARION E. CARL ESTABLISHES ALTITUDE RECORD. In 1953, NATC Pax River test pilot Marion E. Carl established a new world's altitude record of 83,000 feet while test-flying the Douglas D-558 Phase II Skyrocket above Edwards AFB, California. In this photograph, Carl is piloting the Skyrocket, which has been dropped from the bomb bay of a Navy P2B-1 mothercraft. The Skyrocket was designed to further explore the supersonic flight realm. (NASA.)

VR-1 Receives First R7V-1 Polaris. Shown here is the christening ceremony for VR-1's first R7V-1 Polaris at NAS Pax River on March 6, 1953. Important guests present include, from left to right, Lt. S. Goldstein, Lt. M. Hughes, Lieutenant Lenihan, Comdr. E. Quinn, Comdr. L.S. Collins, Capt. J.S. McClure, Rear Adm. A.M. Pride (chief of the Bureau of Aeronautics, 1947–1951, and commander of NATC Pax River, 1952–1953), Capt. J.T. Taylor, Captain Hancock, Capt. S.A. Vanevery Jr., Capt. M.M. Cloukey, and Capt. I.L. Dew, among others. (US National Archives, Still Pictures Branch.)

McDonnell XF3H-1 Demon Prototype. A McDonnell XF3H-1 Demon prototype awaits flight trials at NATC Pax River on August 11, 1953. One of the Demon's shortcomings was that it was underpowered. Production versions of the Demon, designated F3H-2s with more powerful engines, were fleet operational throughout the 1950s and, together with the McDonnell F4H-1 Phantom II, formed the Navy's fleet-defender force during the Cuban Missile Crisis. The Demon was officially retired from fleet duty in 1965. (US National Archives, Still Pictures Branch.)

NAVALIZED SABRE PROTOTYPE. A North American XFJ-2B Fury prototype, a navalized version of the famous USAF F-86 Sabre, is shown before flight trials at NATC Pax River on August 18, 1953. Furies remained fleet operational with the Navy until the late 1950s. (US National Archives, Still Pictures Branch.)

TRACKER CARRIER-BASED ASW AIRCRAFT. The Grumman XS2F-1 Tracker served as the Navy's primary carrier-based ASW aircraft until 1980, when it was replaced by the jet-powered Lockheed S-3A Viking. This Tracker carrier-based ASW aircraft prototype is shown at NAS Pax River on August 19, 1953. (US National Archives, Still Pictures Branch.)

Neptune Smokeless JATO Flight Test. A Lockheed P2V Neptune patrol bomber performs a smokeless JATO flight test at NAS Pax River in August 1953. (US National Archives, Still Pictures Branch.)

Neptune Smoke JATO Flight Test. A Lockheed P2V Neptune patrol bomber performs a smoke JATO flight test at NAS Pax River in August 1953. (US National Archives, Still Pictures Branch.)

FLEXIBLE LANDING DECK. Aircraft performed simulated arrested carrier landings on a flexible landing deck. The deck at NAS Pax River is seen here on February 7, 1955. (US National Archives, Still Pictures Branch.)

TRADEWIND FLYING BOAT. The Convair R3Y Tradewind flying boat arrives at NAS Pax River for flight- and fleet-suitability trials on February 24, 1955. Civilian test pilot Donald Germeroad is at the controls. The Tradewind benefited from design data obtained from flight tests of a captured World War II German Blohm & Voss BV-222 Wiking ("Viking") flying boat at NATC Pax River following the war. (US National Archives, Still Pictures Branch.)

SEDUCTIVE SKYRAY. The XF4D-1 Skyray, prototype of the F4D-1 Skyray series, was an advanced tailless jet fleet defender design. The aircraft underwent substantive flight-testing at NATC Pax River before undergoing carrier trials aboard the USS *Coral Sea* in the waters near Virginia in October 1953. After undergoing an engine upgrade, the Skyray became the Navy's first fleet defender to penetrate the sound barrier. This photograph was taken at NATC Pax River on March 8, 1955. (US National Archives, Still Pictures Branch.)

SEAMASTER PROTOTYPE. The Martin XP6M-1 SeaMaster, designed for the Navy as a high-speed minelayer and nuclear bomber, was extensively flight-tested at NAS Pax River. This SeaMaster prototype jet-powered flying boat is in flight over southern Maryland on January 31, 1958. (US Navy.)

Fury In-Flight Refueling Test. Here, two North American FJ-4Bs of the Service Test Division, NATC Pax River, perform an in-flight refueling test above southern Maryland on April 23, 1958. The aircraft are using their North American in-flight refueling buddy stores. (US National Archives, Still Pictures Branch.)

SKYHAWK IN-FLIGHT REFUELING TEST. These Douglas YA4D-2 Skyhawks of the Service Test Division, NATC Pax River, are also shown during an in-flight refueling test above southern Maryland on April 23, 1958. The aircraft are using Douglas in-flight refueling buddy stores. (US National Archives, Still Pictures Branch.)

Four

ADVENT OF THE MODERN JET AGE AND THE AMERICAN EFFORT IN VIETNAM
1961–1975

The turbulent 1960s and 1970s saw the advent of the modern jet age and America's participation in the Vietnam War, a war that ultimately became a prolonged and unsuccessful struggle to contain the spread of communism in Southeast Asia. The war featured the use of new advanced attack aircraft, such as the Douglas A-4 Skyhawk, Grumman A-6A Intruder, and Vought A-7A Corsair II. Advanced versions of the A-1 Skyraider, essentially a piston-engine attack aircraft holdover from the Korean War, were used extensively by the US Navy, with one Skyraider even scoring an aerial victory over a much faster North Vietnamese Mig-17 Fresco subsonic fighter jet. Advanced supersonic fighters, such as the Vought F-8 Crusader and McDonnell Douglas F-4 Phantom II, were introduced into combat. NAS Patuxent River played an important role, conducting the fleet-acceptance and carrier trials of these aircraft and their associated weapons tests.

The 1960s and early 1970s also saw the advent of America's highly successful space program, which enabled the nation to win the space race with the Soviet Union. Graduates of the USNTPS, and NATC veterans, became NASA astronauts, playing key roles in this historic achievement.

In 1972, Pax River began flight-testing a powerful, advanced swing-wing fleet defender that became known as the Grumman F-14A Tomcat. Although it entered the Navy fleet too late to see combat in the Vietnam War, the Tomcat went on to become an outstanding fleet warrior in future conflicts over the Gulf of Sidra and in the Persian Gulf, Iraq, and Afghanistan.

FUTURE MIG-KILLER. A McDonnell Douglas F-4H Phantom II prototype undergoes flight- and fleet-suitability trials above NATC Pax River on February 16, 1961. The Phantom II would go on to serve as a major MiG-killer in the Vietnam War and excel as a fighter/bomber in ground-attack missions. The Phantom II was retired from active fleet duty in the 1980s. (US National Archives, Still Pictures Branch.)

FIRST AMERICAN IN SPACE. TPS graduate and NASA astronaut Alan B. Shepard (USN) is seen in the Mercury spacecraft *Freedom 7* prior to making his historic dash into space on May 5, 1961. (NASA.)

First American to Orbit Earth. TPS graduate and NASA astronaut John H. Glenn Jr. (USMC) boards his Mercury spacecraft, *Friendship 7*, en route to becoming the first American to orbit the Earth in 1962. (NASA.)

TPS Graduate John Glenn. NASA Mercury astronaut John H. Glenn Jr. poses in his Mercury-era space suit in 1962. (NASA.)

CARRIER-BASED RECONNAISSANCE/NUCLEAR ATTACK JET CARRIER TRIALS. A North American A3J-1 Vigilante prototype, a supersonic, carrier-based reconnaissance/nuclear attack jet, is prepared for carrier trials onboard the USS *Saratoga* (CVA-60) in the early 1960s. Comdr. Carl Cruse, Lt. Comdr. Ed Decker, and Lt. Dick Wright crewed the aircraft during the trials. The Vigilante prototype has been restored and is currently on display at NAS Pax River. (US Navy.)

INTRUDER PROTOTYPE AND ORDNANCE. A Grumman A-6A Intruder all-weather attack bomber prototype and its array of weapons ordnance are shown in 1962. From the early 1960s until 1996, the Intruder underwent extensive flight- and weapons-testing at NAS Pax River. The Intruder served the Navy and Marine Corps from the mid-1960s until 1996, seeing its first combat during the Vietnam War. Among the weapons shown here are Bullpup air-to-ground missiles and iron gravity bombs. (US Navy.)

F-4B PHANTOM II. A McDonnell Douglas F-4B Phantom II makes an arrested landing approach at NATC Pax River's Mark 7 site in 1969. At this testing site, a catapult and arresting gear are used to routinely perform simulated aircraft carrier trials prior to fleet acceptance. (US National Archives, Still Pictures Branch.)

QH-50D DASH DRONE HELICOPTER. A QH-50D Dash drone helicopter undergoes flight trials above NAS Pax River on February 12, 1970. The rotorcraft is carrying two torpedoes. (US National Archives, Still Pictures Branch.)

TPS Graduate on the Moon. Apollo 14 mission commander and TPS graduate Alan B. Shepard (USN) poses next to the American flag for a photograph taken during his extravehicular activity (EVA) on the Moon in early 1971. Shepard also hit golf balls on the lunar surface with a makeshift club. (NASA.)

Marine Corps Jump Jet. A McDonnell Douglas AV-8A Harrier vertical/short takeoff and landing (V/STOL) jump jet performs a vertical takeoff during flight trials at NAS Pax River in July 1971. The AV-8A and its later variant, the AV-8B Harrier II, both built by McDonnell Douglas, were Americanized versions of the famous British Hawker Siddeley Harrier jump jet. AV-8B Harrier IIs served the Marine Corps well during Operations Desert Storm, Iraqi Freedom, and Enduring Freedom. (US National Archives, Still Pictures Branch.)

RECORD-SETTING ORION. A Project Magnet Lockheed RP-3D Orion of Oceanographic Development Squadron Eight (VXN-8) is seen at NAS Pax River on November 4, 1972, after successfully completing a record-setting 16.5-hour, 2,450-nautical-mile flight to monitor the magnetism of the North Pole. (US National Archives, Still Pictures Branch.)

F-14A TOMCAT. A Grumman F-14A Tomcat prototype, assigned to NATC Pax River, undergoes carrier trials aboard the USS *Forrestal* (CVA-59) off the Virginia coast in November 1973. The aircraft also performed a weapons flight test of an AIM-54 Phoenix long-range air-to-air missile. The missile is visible on a pylon under the fuselage of the aircraft. (US National Archives, Still Pictures Branch.)

LOCKHEED S-3A VIKING. An Air Test and Evaluation Squadron One, VX-1, Lockheed S-3A Viking carrier-based ASW aircraft is prepared for carrier-suitability trials at NAS Pax River on May 28, 1974. The Viking was developed as a replacement for the aging Grumman S-2 Tracker in the carrier-based ASW role. (US National Archives, Still Pictures Branch.)

INTRUDER AND CRUISE MISSILE. A Grumman A-6A Intruder, with a Navy YBGM-110 Cruise Missile Aerodynamic Test Vehicle (ATV) mounted on an underwing pylon, awaits a special-weapons flight test at NAS Pax River in November 1974. (US National Archives, Still Pictures Branch.)

Five

PAX HELPS AMERICA
WIN THE COLD WAR
AND ESTABLISH
SUPERPOWER SUPREMACY
1976–1999

Following America's departure from Vietnam in 1975, military planners and aerospace industry officials labored to help return the country to a position of military strength to meet any threat thrown at it by the Soviet Union and its satellite communist states. In 1980, the USSR invaded Afghanistan, and the global perception of America was one of failure and weakness. In addition, Libya's mercurial dictator, Col. Muammar Gaddafi, continually precipitated confrontations with the United States in the 1980s. In 1990, Iraq's Saddam Hussein ordered his military forces to invade Kuwait. America and its coalition allies responded with a massive military buildup of their own in the form of Operation Desert Shield. In January 1991, Operation Desert Storm, the mission to eject Iraqi forces from Kuwait, commenced under the authorization of Pres. George H.W. Bush. The American military was eager to erase the memories of Vietnam and, with the help of its coalition partners, routed Iraqi military forces. All of the Navy and Marine Corps aircraft and rotorcraft participating in these conflicts were at one time flight-tested and evaluated at NAS Patuxent River.

In the early 1990s, a globally unique aircraft test and simulation facility became operational at Pax River. It has made a tremendous difference in preparing Navy and Marine Corps aviators and aircraft for combat. This installation, known as the Air Combat Environment Test and Evaluation Facility (ACETEF), houses several departments, including the Aircraft Anechoic Test Facility (AATF), where aircraft undergo electronic warfare simulation testing, as well as several aircraft air-combat simulators.

Pursuit of the "peace through strength" philosophy and tremendous buildup of the US military initiated by Pres. Ronald Reagan in 1980 and maintained by President George H.W. Bush from 1988 to 1991 forced the USSR to increase its military spending to match America's overwhelming military might. As a result, this American philosophy and policy ultimately bankrupted the Soviet Union and brought about its demise in December 1991. Consequently, America won the Cold War against the USSR and achieved superpower supremacy, and NAS Pax River played a crucial role in making this happen.

EA-6B Prowler. The Grumman EA-6B Prowler served the Navy and Marine Corps as a primary carrier-based electronic countermeasures aircraft since the late 1970s. This Prowler awaits flight trials at NATC Pax River on August 9, 1977. (US National Archives, Still Pictures Branch.)

Pax River Hangars. The Flight Test Hangars at NAS Pax River are seen here in November 1977. Visible are a Lockheed C-130 Hercules transport in the foreground and several Lockheed P-3C Orion ASW patrol aircraft in the background. (US National Archives, Still Pictures Branch.)

SPECIAL ELECTRONICS ORION. A Lockheed EP-3A Orion is seen at NAS Pax River in March 1978. The EP-3As were used by the Navy to monitor antenna radiation patterns of radars aboard US ships. (US National Archives, Still Pictures Branch.)

AIR EXPO '78 STATIC DISPLAY. This is a view of Air Expo '78 at NAS Pax River on September 9, 1978. Among the aircraft shown here are, in no particular order, a P-3C Orion, S-3A Viking, A-3B Skywarrior, E-2C Hawkeye, EA-6B Prowler, OV-10A Bronco, UH-2B Seasprite, F-14A Tomcat, F-4J Phantom II, YA-7E Corsair II, A-7E Corsair II, A-6E Intruder, A-4F Skyhawk, and an AV-8A Harrier. (US National Archives, Still Pictures Branch.)

NORTHROP **YF-17** PROTOTYPE. A YF-17 is on static display at Air Expo '78 at NAS Pax River on September 9, 1978. (US National Archives, Still Pictures Branch.)

PHANTOM **II** ARRESTED LANDING. A McDonnell Douglas F-4B Phantom II performs an arrested landing at the USS *Enterprise Jr.* at NAS Pax River in January 1979. The *Enterprise Jr.* was a "concrete carrier," or simulated flight deck, of America's first nuclear-powered aircraft carrier, the USS *Enterprise* (CVN-65). This simulated deck was also used to assess carrier visual-landing aids. (US National Archives, Still Pictures Branch.)

LAST NAVY PHANTOM II VARIANT. On January 14, 1979, this NATC Pax River McDonnell Douglas F-4S Phantom II performed carrier trials aboard the USS *Kitty Hawk* (CV-63) in the Pacific Ocean. The F-4S was the last Phantom II variant to enter fleet service with the Navy. (US National Archives, Still Pictures Branch.)

HARRIER II SKI-JUMP FLIGHT TEST. A Marine Corps YAV-8B Harrier II jump-jet prototype makes a ski-jump takeoff at Pax River on July 1, 1979. (US Marine Corps.)

Hornet Flight and Weapons Trials. A McDonnell Douglas F/A-18 Hornet prototype, carrying AIM-9 Sidewinder air-to-air missiles (wingtips) and AIM-7 Sparrow air-to-air missiles (inboard), undergoes flight- and weapons trials above NATC Pax River in November 1979. The Hornet was developed as an advanced strike fighter for the Navy and Marine Corps, replacing the LTV A-7E Corsair II in the carrier-based attack role. The Hornet has served, and continues to serve, as a primary air-superiority fighter. (US National Archives, Still Pictures Branch.)

Hornet Flight Tests. Here, two F/A-18 Hornet prototypes, carrying AIM-9 Sidewinder air-to-air missiles, perform a test flight above NATC Pax River in May 1980. This photograph was shot from the backseat of a two-seat Hornet prototype. (US National Archives, Still Pictures Branch.)

SEAHAWK PROTOTYPE. A Sikorsky SH-60B Seahawk ASW helicopter prototype awaits flight trials at NAS Pax River on May 1, 1981. (US Navy photograph by Jim Kellar.)

HELICOPTER COUNTERMEASURES FLIGHT TEST. A Pax River–based Sikorsky CH-53D Sea Stallion drops flares in a countermeasures test over the waters off southern Maryland on July 1, 1982. (US Navy photograph by Vernon Pugh.)

AERIAL REFUELING FLIGHT TESTS. An NATC Pax River Convair UC-880 performs in-flight refueling of a NATC Pax River F-4 Phantom II on September 3, 1986. A TPS TA-4J Skyhawk stands by (background), while an NATC Pax River A-6 Intruder (bottom foreground) waits a turn at in-flight refueling. (US National Archives, Still Pictures Branch.)

INTRUDER CARRIER-SUITABILITY TESTS. A NATC Pax River A-6E advanced Intruder, equipped with a TRAM nose turret, performs an arrested landing aboard the USS *Dwight D. Eisenhower* (CVN-69) on June 16, 1987. Carrier-based A-6Es participated in Operation El Dorado Canyon (attack on Libya) and Operation Desert Storm. The Intruder was retired from fleet service in 1996. (US National Archives, Still Pictures Branch.)

VX-1 Orion Flyover. A Pax River–based VX-1 Lockheed P-3C Orion ASW patrol aircraft is seen in flight over NAS Pax River in the early 1990s. (US Navy.)

Enhanced Performance Engines Hornet. An NATC Pax River Convair UC-880 performs an in-flight refueling test of the Enhanced Performance Engines (EPE) F/A-18A Hornet test aircraft on November 1, 1991. The Hornet was outfitted with F404-GE-402 EPE. The UC-880 was used by the NATC in Tomahawk cruise-missile tests as well as in developing better methods for in-flight refueling of aircraft. (US National Archives, Still Pictures Branch.)

TOMCAT AIR-TO-GROUND CAPABILITY FLIGHT TEST. A Naval Air Warfare Center Aircraft Division (NAWCAD) F-14A/B Tomcat performs an air launch of the Tactical Air Launched Decoy (TALD) as part of an air-to-ground capability flight test on February 1, 1994. More than a decade earlier and again toward the end of the 1980s, the Tomcat demonstrated its air superiority and fleet-defender prowess by dispatching two Libyan Sukhoi Su-22 Fitter and MiG-23 Flogger interceptors in separate incidents over the Gulf of Sidra. (US National Archives, Still Pictures Branch.)

WALLEYE II GLIDE BOMB FLIGHT TEST. A NAWCAD A-6E Intruder performs a weapons flight test of a Walleye II TV-guided glide bomb at the Naval Air Warfare Center (NAWC) Pax River in February 1994. (US Navy photograph by Vernon Pugh.)

SH-60F Seahawk Hellfire Missile Weapons Flight Test. A NAWCAD Sikorsky SH-60F Seahawk helicopter launches a Hellfire air-to-ground missile at a target in a weapons flight test over the Patuxent River on March 1, 1995. (US National Archives, Still Pictures Branch.)

The "Bombcat." A Strike Division F-14 Tomcat based at NAS Pax River performs a laser-guided bomb drop test in the early 1990s. The Tomcat became so precise and proficient at bombing that its pilots affectionately dubbed it the "Bombcat." The Tomcat was retired from the Navy's fleet in 2006. (US Navy.)

ANECHOIC CAVERN. In the early 1990s, the Air Combat Environment Test and Evaluation Facility (ACETEF) became operational at NAS Pax River. This center houses several facilities, including the Aircraft Anechoic Test Facility (AATF), the inside of which is shown here. A Grumman EA-6B Prowler and McDonnell Douglas F/A-18C have been strategically positioned for electronic warfare simulation testing in the chamber. (US Navy.)

HARRISON FORD AT NAS PAX RIVER. The actor Harrison Ford signs autographs at NAS Pax River at the nose of an F-18 Hornet on September 25, 1998. Ford took time out from filming his movie *Random Hearts*, which features scenes at the naval air station. (US National Archives, Still Pictures Branch.)

Six

MAINTAINING THE EDGE
2000–2014

Since the beginning of the new millennium in 2001, NAS Patuxent River has worked to help modernize America's naval air arm to 21st-century technological standards and keep the nation a step ahead of potential adversaries. Flight-testing and evaluation of advanced Navy and Marine Corps high-performance jet aircraft has continued, including fleet-acceptance and carrier trials of the Boeing F/A-18E and F/A-18F Super Hornet, Boeing E/A-18G Growler, and the stealthy Lockheed Martin F-35 Lightning II Joint Strike Fighter (JSF). The JSF is intended to replace 30-plus-year-old Boeing F/A-18C strike fighters. Flight-testing and evaluation were conducted of advanced rotorcraft, including advanced versions of the venerable Huey Cobra gunship and UH-1 Huey, and the V-22 Osprey tilt-rotor wonder. Flight-testing and evaluation of advanced unmanned aerial vehicles (UAVs) continued as well, including successful carrier trials of the future of naval aviation, in the form of the jet-powered Northrop Grumman X-47B Unmanned Combat Air System (UCAS).

Today, NAS Pax River is the location for the headquarters of the Naval Air Systems Command (NAVAIR), formed in 1966 to facilitate and support naval aviation operations. NAS Pax River is also the home of the Naval Air Warfare Center Aircraft Division (NAWCAD), which has grown to include the US Naval Test Pilot School, Naval Strike Aircraft Test Squadron (VX-23), Naval Force Aircraft Test Squadron (VX-20), and the Naval Rotary Wing Aircraft Test Squadron (HX¬21). These elite training and test groups routinely fly a total of 140 aircraft, consisting of 40 different variants.

Pod Away! A Boeing VX-23 F/A-18C Hornet drops Mk-83 1,000-pound bombs during an Advanced Targeting Forward Looking Infrared (ATFLIR) adjacent stores drop test at the Atlantic Range in 2002. (US Navy photograph by Vernon Pugh.)

Super Hornet Carrier Trials. An Air Test and Evaluation Squadron VX-23 Salty Dogs Boeing F/A-18E Super Hornet, based at NAS Pax River, is shown during carrier-trial operations from the USS *Theodore Roosevelt* in 2002. (US Navy photograph by Photographer's Mate 2nd Class Angela M. Virnig.)

OMNIPRESENT OSPREY. A NAVAIR Bell Boeing V-22 Integrated Test Team (ITT) Marine Corps Osprey performs a test flight over Pax River in 2002. The Osprey represents the state of the art in tilt-rotor design and provides the Marine Corps with rapid global deployment capability of ground forces. This capability was used to great effect in Operation Iraqi Freedom and is currently being used in Operation Enduring Freedom in Afghanistan. The aircraft is shown here in the conventional flight mode. (US Navy photograph by Vernon Pugh.)

HAWKEYE WITH ADVANCED PROPULSION. A Northrop Grumman E-2C Hawkeye outfitted with advanced composite eight-bladed propellers is shown on its first test flight at Pax River. (US Navy photograph by Vernon Pugh.)

HERCULES/ADVANCED HAWKEYE TEST BED. In 2002, the Navy flew this Lockheed Martin NC-130H Hercules at Pax River on flight tests to prove a state-of-the-art radar system for advanced versions of the Northrop Grumman E-2C Hawkeye. (US Navy.)

SEA STALLION TEST FLIGHT. A Sikorsky CH-53D Sea Stallion descends for touchdown at Pax River. (US Navy.)

VECTORED FLIGHT TEST BED. In 2003, the X-31 VECTOR experimental research aircraft successfully completed a 24-degree angle-of-attack, extremely short takeoff-and-landing approach at Pax River. The X-31 testbed utilizes the latest advances in thrust-vectoring technology to demonstrate advanced maneuvering and takeoff-and-landing, high-performance fighter capabilities. The VECTOR program is a cooperative research effort between the Federal Republic of Germany and the United States. (US Navy photograph by James Darcy.)

SUPER HORNET CARRIER TRIALS. A two-seat Boeing F/A-18F Super Hornet of VX-23 Salty Dogs, based at Pax River, with hook down and gear down, performs an arrested landing during carrier trials on the USS *Ronald Reagan* (CVN-76) in 2003. (US Navy photograph by Photographer's Mate Second Class Chad McNeeley.)

VIKING UPGRADE. An advanced NAVAIR VX-1 Lockheed S-3B Viking ASW/tanker aircraft, the sole S-3B left based at Pax River, performed a successful carrier-feasibility test, making an arrested landing at Pax River in September 2004. This aircraft was outfitted with a Mass Memory Unit (MMU) for enhanced flight-data retention. MMU-equipped S-3Bs were later integrated into the fleet. (US Navy photograph by Rebecca March.)

ADVANCED ANTI-RADIATION GUIDED MISSILE (AARGM) FLIGHT TEST. A Pax River–based VX-23 Salty Dogs Boeing F/A-18F Super Hornet armed with AARGMs is seen here on a flight test. The AARGM is used for Surface-to-Air Missile (SAM) site suppression. (US Navy photograph by Greg L. Davis.)

NAVAL AVIATOR TRAINING MAINSTAY. A TPS North American T-2C Buckeye performs a training flight over Pax River in 2005. From 1959, the Buckeye served as the Navy's primary trainer until it was retired in 2008 in favor of the T-45 Goshawk. (US Navy photograph by Photographer's Mate Second Class Daniel J. McLain.)

CAYUSE HELO TRAINING FLIGHT. A TPS TH-6B Cayuse helicopter lifts off from Pax River on a training flight. (US Navy photograph by Photographer's Mate Second Class Daniel J. McLain.)

TALON TRAINING FLIGHT. A TPS Northrop T-38A Talon lifts off from NAS Pax River on a training mission. TPS is dedicated to the study and conception of new flight-test methods and training with advanced flight technologies. (US Navy photograph by Photographer's Mate Second Class Daniel J. McLain.)

HORNET TRAINING FLIGHT. A TPS F/A-18B goes gear up for a training mission in 2005. TPS flies 50 aircraft consisting of 13 different types. (US Navy photograph by Photographer's Mate Second Class Daniel J. McLain.)

TPS Graduate Space Shuttle Pilot. The crew of Space Shuttle *Discovery* STS-121 poses in 2006. Capt. Mark E. Kelly (third from right), a graduate of TPS at Pax, served as the pilot for the mission. (NASA.)

EA-18G Growler. The Boeing EA-18G Growler was developed as a replacement for the aging EA-6B Prowler, to serve as the primary electronic warfare/attack aircraft for the Navy and Marine Corps. Here, an EA-18G prototype of VX-23 Salty Dogs performs a test flight over Pax River in 2006. (US Navy.)

ADVANCED COBRA HELICOPTER GUNSHIP. A Bell AH-1Z Cobra helicopter gunship of Pax River's Rotary Wing Aircraft Test Squadron (HX)-21 prepares to land on the USS *Wasp* (LHD-1) after performing a test flight. The AH-1Z features a four-bladed rotor for enhanced maneuverability and stability. (US Navy photograph by Mass Communication Specialist First Class Rebekah Adler.)

PUBLIC ADDRESS BY SECRETARY OF THE NAVY. During a visit to NAS Pax River on September 1, 2011, the Secretary of the Navy, Ray Mabus, commended the Blue Angels and their use of a new biofuel in performing aerial demonstrations. (US Navy photograph by Chief Mass Communications Specialist Sam Shavers.)

BLUE ANGELS FORM UP. The Navy's premier aerial demonstration team, the Blue Angels, form up during an aerial demonstration at the Naval Air Station Patuxent River Air Expo, held on September 3, 2011. (US Navy photograph by Mass Communication Specialist Second Class Kiona Miller.)

GREEN OSPREY. A Bell Boeing MV-22 Osprey makes a vertical takeoff at Pax River in 2011 on a flight to test the feasibility of a new biofuel. (US Navy photograph by Steven Kays.)

GREEN PROWLER. A VX-23 Salty Dogs Grumman EA-6B Prowler performs a biofuel feasibility flight test at Pax River in 2011. (US Navy photograph by Kelly Schindler.)

FUTURE ASW WARRIOR. A Boeing P-8A Poseidon performs a simulated MK-54 Torpedo drop over Pax River. The Poseidon was designed as a replacement for the aging Lockheed P-3C Orion ASW patrol aircraft. (US Navy photograph by Greg L. Davis.)

FUTURE FLEET DEFENDER. The Navy is conducting extensive flight tests of the Lockheed Martin F-35C Lightning II Joint Strike Fighter (JSF) at Pax River. The JSF is intended to serve the Navy as a primary fleet defender well into the future. (US Navy photograph courtesy of Lockheed Martin.)

JSF LASER-GUIDED BOMB DROP TEST. A Lockheed Martin F-35B Lightning II JSF test aircraft, piloted by Capt. Michael Kingen, performs a laser-guided bomb drop test at Pax River. The F-35B is the Marine Corps Short Takeoff Vertical Landing (STOVL) version of the JSF. (Lockheed Martin by Dane Wiedmann.)

FUTURE OF NAVAL AVIATION. The Northrop Grumman X-47B Unmanned Combat Air System (UCAS) is shown high in flight above NAS Pax River on its maiden test flight on July 29, 2012. (US Navy.)

DESTINATION: HISTORY. The Northrop Grumman X-47B UCAS takes off from NAS Pax River, headed for its historic destination—an arrested landing aboard the carrier USS *George H.W. Bush* (CVN-77) on July 10, 2013. (US Navy.)

UCAS Carrier Trials. On July 10, 2013, the Northrop Grumman X-47B UCAS made a successful arrested landing on the USS *George H.W. Bush* (CVN-77) off the Virginia coast. The plane had taken off from NAS Pax River. The event marked the first time in history that an unmanned jet-powered aircraft made a successful arrested landing aboard an aircraft carrier. (US Navy photograph by Capt. Jane E. Campbell.)

DISCOVER THOUSANDS OF LOCAL HISTORY BOOKS
FEATURING MILLIONS OF VINTAGE IMAGES

Arcadia Publishing, the leading local history publisher in the United States, is committed to making history accessible and meaningful through publishing books that celebrate and preserve the heritage of America's people and places.

Find more books like this at
www.arcadiapublishing.com

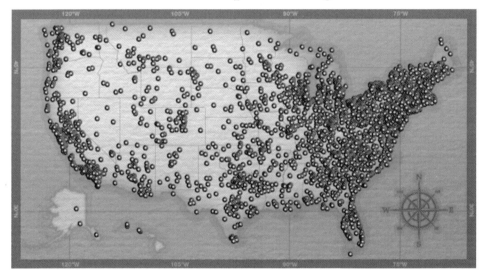

Search for your hometown history, your old stomping grounds, and even your favorite sports team.

Consistent with our mission to preserve history on a local level, this book was printed in South Carolina on American-made paper and manufactured entirely in the United States. Products carrying the accredited Forest Stewardship Council (FSC) label are printed on 100 percent FSC-certified paper.